Cambodia

Countries of the World

by Monika Davies

BELLWETHER MEDIA • MINNEAPOLIS, MN

Blastoff! Readers are carefully developed by literacy experts to build reading stamina and move students toward fluency by combining standards-based content with developmentally appropriate text.

Level 1 provides the most support through repetition of high-frequency words, light text, predictable sentence patterns, and strong visual support.

Level 2 offers early readers a bit more challenge through varied sentences, increased text load, and text-supportive special features.

Level 3 advances early-fluent readers toward fluency through increased text load, less reliance on photos, advancing concepts, longer sentences, and more complex special features.

★ Blastoff! Universe

Reading Level

- Blastoff! Beginners — Grade K
- Blastoff! Readers — Grades 1–3
- Blastoff! Discovery — Grade 4

This edition first published in 2024 by Bellwether Media, Inc.

No part of this publication may be reproduced in whole or in part without written permission of the publisher. For information regarding permission, write to Bellwether Media, Inc., Attention: Permissions Department, 6012 Blue Circle Drive, Minnetonka, MN 55343.

Library of Congress Cataloging-in-Publication Data

LC record for Cambodia available at: https://lccn.loc.gov/2023046584

Text copyright © 2024 by Bellwether Media, Inc. BLASTOFF! READERS and associated logos are trademarks and/or registered trademarks of Bellwether Media, Inc.

Editor: Rachael Barnes   Series Design: Gabriel Hilger   Book Designer: Kathleen Petelinsek
Printed in the United States of America, North Mankato, MN.

Table of Contents

All About Cambodia	4
Land and Animals	6
Life in Cambodia	12
Cambodia Facts	20
Glossary	22
To Learn More	23
Index	24

All About Cambodia

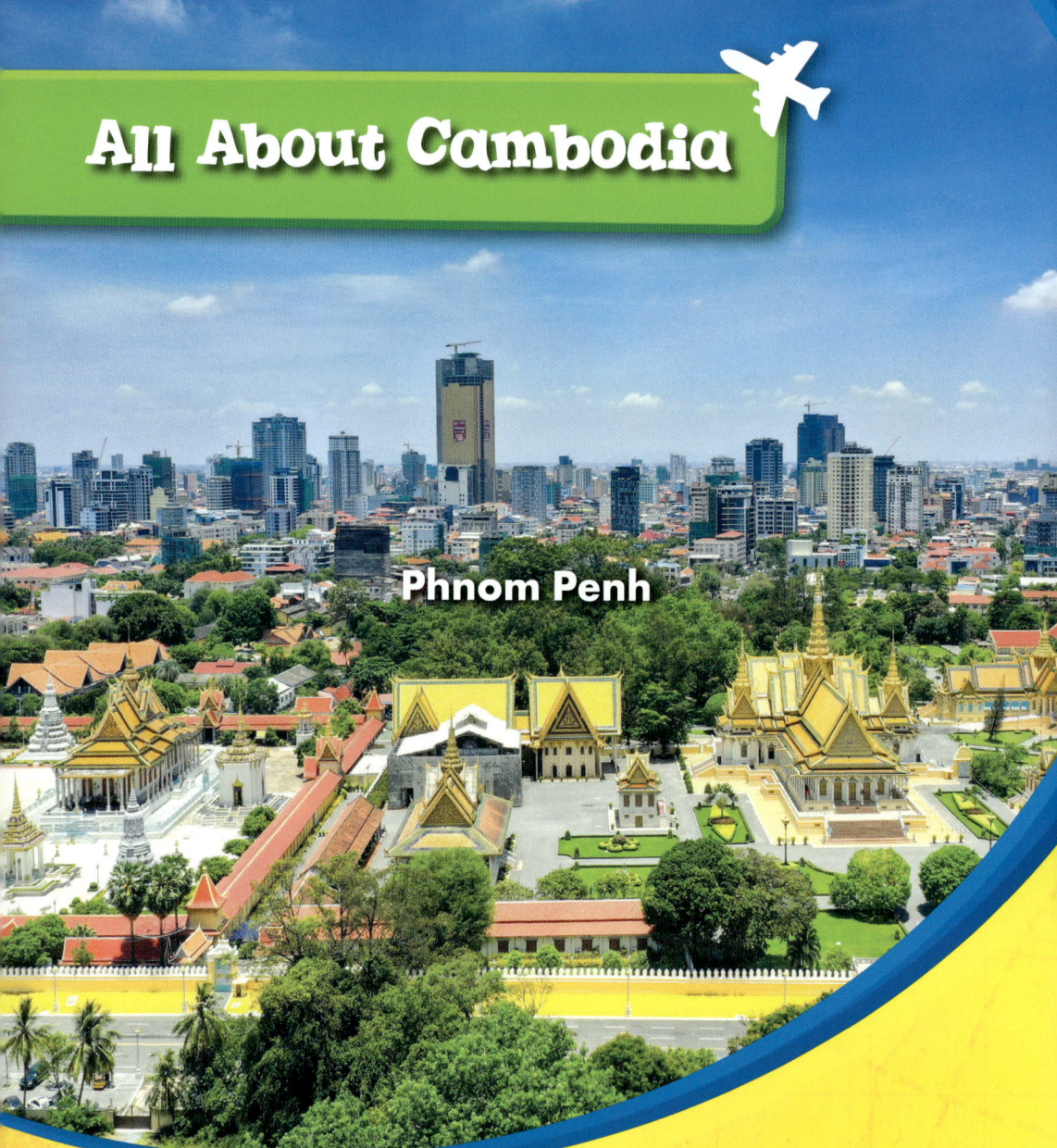

Phnom Penh

Cambodia is in Southeast Asia. Its capital is Phnom Penh.

The Khmer **Empire** built many of the country's **temples**. Angkor Wat is the most famous.

Land and Animals

Plains spread across central Cambodia. **Rain forests** cover mountains in the southwest.

The Mekong River cuts through the east. It connects to a huge lake.

rain forest

Tonle Sap

Size: up to 6,178 square miles (16,000 square kilometers) during the wet season

Famous For: largest freshwater lake in Southeast Asia

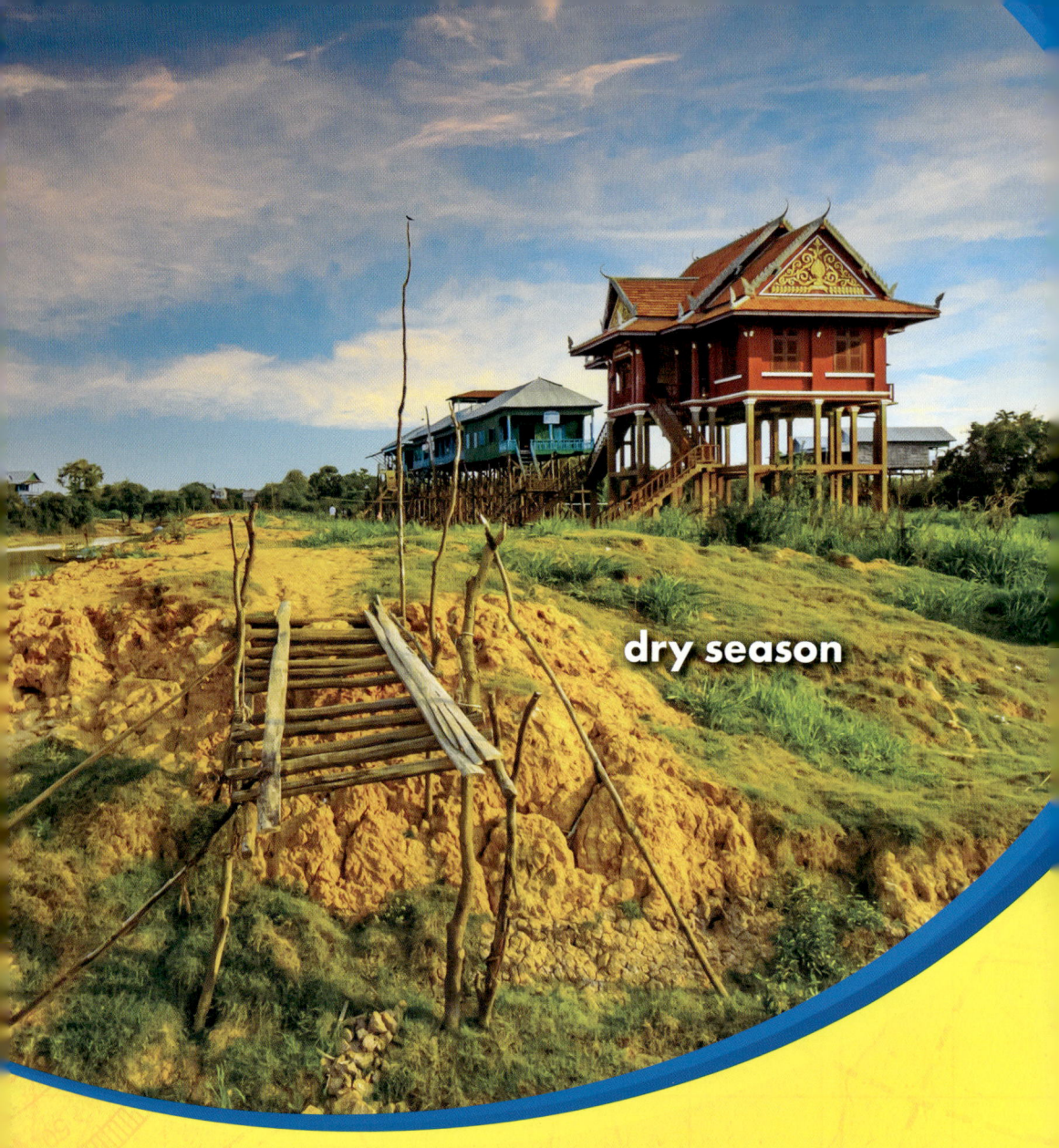

dry season

The country is warm all year. November to April is the dry season.

The wet season is May to October. Rivers and lakes flood.

Tonle Sap during the wet season

Cambodia is full of wildlife. Asian elephants find food in the rain forests. Female king cobras build nests among the trees.

Asian elephant

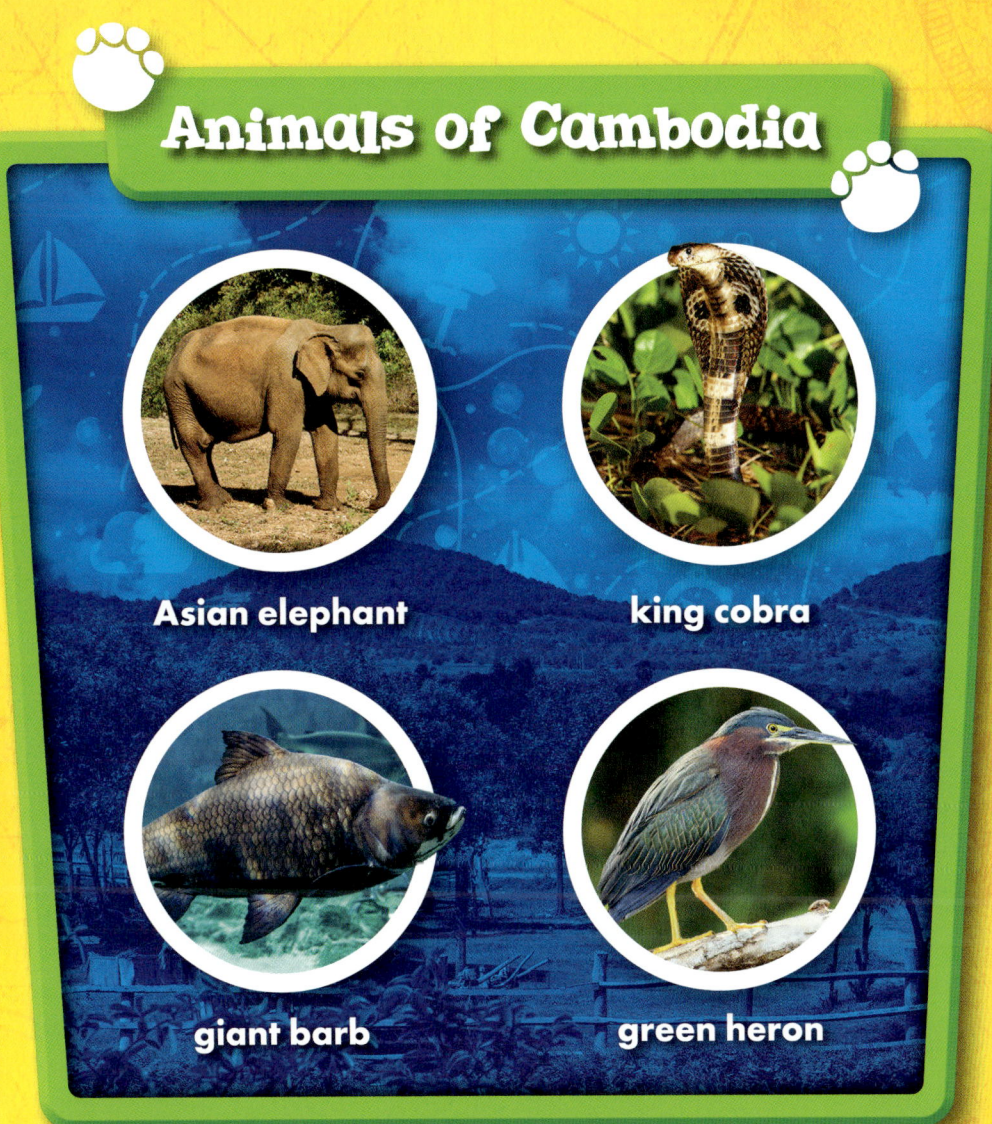

Animals of Cambodia

Asian elephant

king cobra

giant barb

green heron

Giant barbs swim in rivers. Herons fly overhead.

Life in Cambodia

Nearly all Cambodians have a Khmer background. Khmer is the most common language.

People often live in villages. About half of all Cambodians work on farms. Many people practice **Buddhism**.

Angkor Wat Buddhist temple

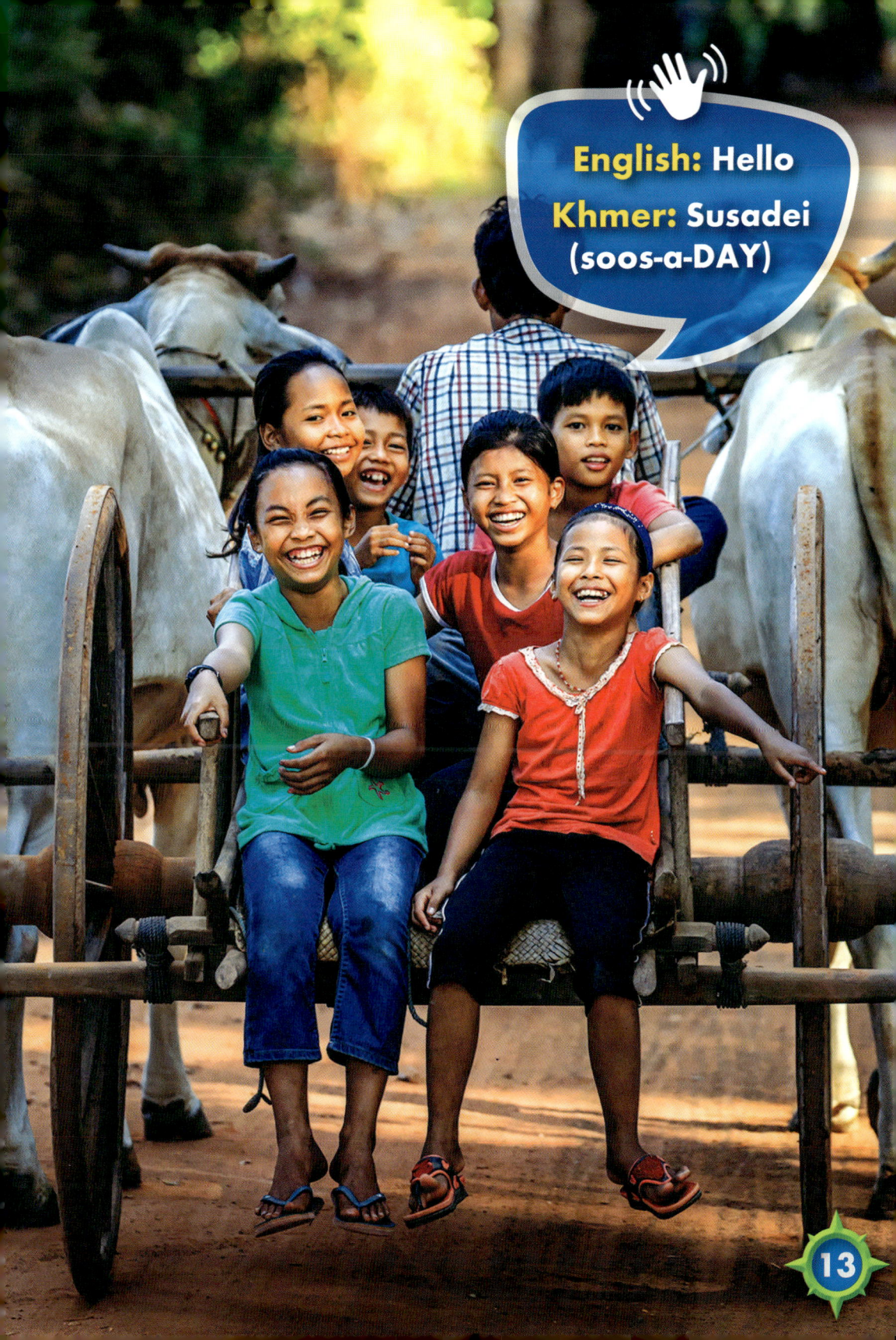

kickboxing

Khmer kickboxing is popular. It is a **martial art**.

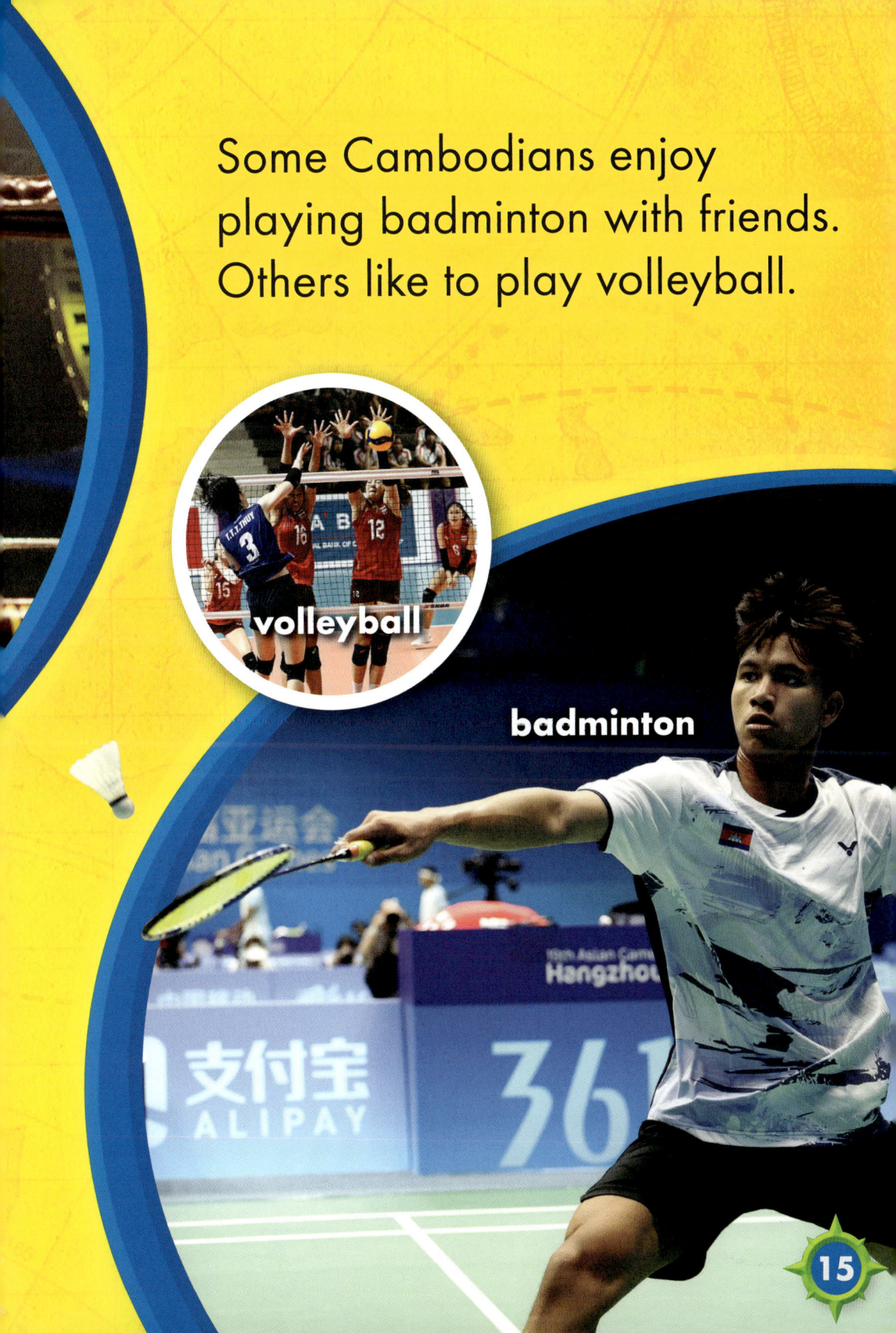

Some Cambodians enjoy playing badminton with friends. Others like to play volleyball.

volleyball

badminton

Rice is a **staple** food. *Amok* is a fish curry. *Num banh chok* is a favorite breakfast.

Cambodian Foods

rice

amok

num banh chok

num ansom

Num ansom is a sticky rice cake. People make it for holidays!

Bon Om Touk is the country's water **festival**. Bright boats race across a river.

Khmer New Year is in April. Families play games and visit temples. Holidays bring Cambodians together!

Khmer New Year

Bon Om Touk

Cambodia Facts

Size:
69,898 square miles
(181,035 square kilometers)

Population:
16,891,245 (2023)

National Holiday:
Independence Day (November 9)

Main Language:
Khmer

Capital City:
Phnom Penh

Famous Face

Name: Loung Ung

Famous For: human rights activist and author

Religions

- Buddhist 97%
- Muslim: 2%
- other 1%

Top Landmarks

Angkor Wat

Banteay Chhmar

Royal Palace

Glossary

Buddhism—a religion of eastern and central Asia based on the teachings of Buddha, the founder of Buddhism

empire—a large area ruled by an emperor

festival—a time or event of celebration

martial art—a sport or skill that first started as a way to fight or stay safe

plains—large areas of flat land

rain forests—thick, green forests that receive a lot of rain

staple—a widely used food or other item

temples—buildings used for religious purposes

To Learn More

AT THE LIBRARY

Kenney, Karen Latchana. *Rain Forests*. Minneapolis, Minn.: Bellwether Media, 2022.

Spanier, Kristine. *Angkor Wat*. Minneapolis, Minn.: Jump!, 2022.

Spanier, Kristine. *Cambodia*. Minneapolis, Minn.: Jump!, 2021.

ON THE WEB

FACTSURFER

Factsurfer.com gives you a safe, fun way to find more information.

1. Go to www.factsurfer.com.
2. Enter "Cambodia" into the search box and click 🔍.
3. Select your book cover to see a list of related content.

Index

Angkor Wat, 5, 12
animals, 10, 11
badminton, 15
Bon Om Touk, 18, 19
Buddhism, 12
Cambodia facts, 20–21
capital (see Phnom Penh)
dry season, 8
farms, 12
flood, 9
food, 10, 16, 17
Khmer, 5, 12, 13, 14, 18
Khmer Empire, 5
Khmer New Year, 18
kickboxing, 14
lake, 6, 7, 9
map, 5
Mekong River, 6
mountains, 6
people, 12, 15, 17, 18
Phnom Penh, 4, 5
plains, 6
rain forests, 6, 10
rivers, 6, 9, 11, 18
say hello, 13
Southeast Asia, 4
temples, 5, 12, 18
Tonle Sap, 7, 9
villages, 12
volleyball, 15
wet season, 9

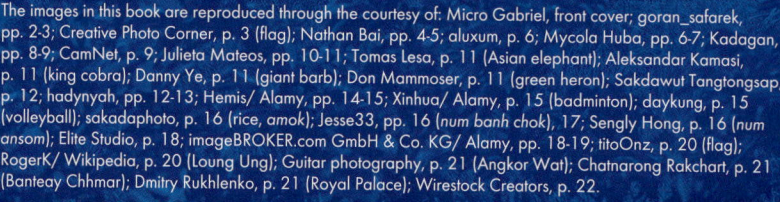

The images in this book are reproduced through the courtesy of: Micro Gabriel, front cover; goran_safarek, pp. 2-3; Creative Photo Corner, p. 3 (flag); Nathan Bai, pp. 4-5; aluxum, p. 6; Mycola Huba, pp. 6-7; Kadagan, pp. 8-9; CamNet, p. 9; Julieta Mateos, pp. 10-11; Tomas Lesa, p. 11 (Asian elephant); Aleksandar Kamasi, p. 11 (king cobra); Danny Ye, p. 11 (giant barb); Don Mammoser, p. 11 (green heron); Sakdawut Tangtongsap, p. 12; hadynyah, pp. 12-13; Hemis/ Alamy, pp. 14-15; Xinhua/ Alamy, p. 15 (badminton); daykung, p. 15 (volleyball); sakadaphoto, p. 16 (rice, *amok*); Jesse33, pp. 16 (*num banh chok*), 17; Sengly Hong, p. 16 (*num ansom*); Elite Studio, p. 18; imageBROKER.com GmbH & Co. KG/ Alamy, pp. 18-19; titoOnz, p. 20 (flag); RogerK/ Wikipedia, p. 20 (Loung Ung); Guitar photography, p. 21 (Angkor Wat); Chatnarong Rakchart, p. 21 (Banteay Chhmar); Dmitry Rukhlenko, p. 21 (Royal Palace); Wirestock Creators, p. 22.